THE MISSING ROLE

Also by Chauntelle Ricks

AVAILABLE NOW

Future Proof: What Every Person and Parent Must Do Before AI Does It For You

COMING SOON

Blended: How to Prepare Your Child for a World School Wasn't Built For

The Missing Role: For Real Estate Brokerages

The Missing Role: For Healthcare

The Missing Role: For Schools

The Missing Role: For Financial Services

THE MISSING ROLE

The Leadership Gap Standing Between Your Team and Real AI Results

Chauntelle Ricks

Certified AI Consultant

Transforming Glory Publishing Group

The Missing Role

The Leadership Gap Standing Between Your Team and Real AI Results

Published in the United States of America

Self-Published, 2026

ISBN: 978-1-962942-12-6 (Paperback)

Library of Congress Control Number: Applied For

Disclaimer:
This book is intended for educational and informational purposes only. The author has made every effort to ensure the accuracy of information at the time of publication. Statistical data and research findings are cited to the best of the author's knowledge. Readers should consult qualified professionals for career, legal, or financial decisions.

Cover design by Chauntelle Ricks

https://stan.store/edgeeffectai

First Edition

Printed in the United States of America

For the leaders who stayed in the room long enough to ask a better question.

A Note Before We Begin

Two months.

That is how fast AI information becomes outdated. Not two years. Not two quarters. Two months. I know this not because I read it in a report, but because I lived it.

Shortly after completing my AI certification, I sat down to review the material I had just studied and realized something that stopped me cold. The landscape had already shifted. Tools had been updated. New capabilities had emerged. Guidance that had been accurate when I started was already incomplete.

Two months. That was all it took.

Now consider this. If a credentialed AI professional, someone actively immersed in this field, can find their knowledge outdated in sixty days, what does that mean for the person your organization hired to lead your AI transition? What does it mean if that person completed a certification program, handed in their final assessment, and has not had a single structured learning update since?

> *It means they are leading your team with a map that no longer matches the territory.*

And it means the adoption gap you are feeling right now, the quiet sense that the investment is in, but the results are not showing up, is not a mystery. It has a name. It has a cause. And it has a solution.

That is what this book is about.

The tools are purchased. The licenses are active. The announcement was made. And almost nothing has changed. You are not imagining it, and you are not alone. This book exists to tell you exactly why, and exactly what to do about it.

— *Chauntelle Ricks*

For the leaders who approved the budget, made the announcement, and are quietly wondering why the needle isn't moving.

CHAPTER ONE

You Are Not Hiring the Wrong People. You Are Hiring for the Wrong Problem.

There is a moment that happens inside almost every organization that has invested in AI. It comes quietly, usually around the six-month mark. The tools are in place. The licenses are active. The person or team responsible for AI is doing something, attending meetings, producing reports, and presenting updates. And yet the work itself, the actual day-to-day work of the people in the organization, looks almost exactly the same as it did before.

That moment is the adoption gap announcing itself.

And when leaders try to diagnose it, the conversation almost always goes in the wrong direction. They ask whether the tools are the right fit. They wonder if the budget was sufficient. They question whether employees are resistant to change. They rarely ask the question that would lead them to the real answer.

Did we hire for the right problem?

> *The job description is written before anyone asks the most important question: what does our organization actually need AI to do for our people?*

Where It All Begins: The Job Description

Before a single candidate applies, before a single resume is reviewed, the adoption gap is often already being created. It is being created inside the job description.

Picture how a typical AI job posting gets written. A senior leader decides the organization needs AI leadership. That request goes to HR or an internal hiring manager. They do what any reasonable professional would do: they look at what other organizations are posting for similar roles. They look at the requested credentials. They look at what the market seems to value. And they write a description that mirrors what they find.

What they find, almost universally, is technical. Engineering backgrounds. Experience deploying AI systems. Knowledge of machine learning frameworks. Prior work in building or implementing AI solutions. These credentials are real and valuable for a specific kind of AI work. But they are often entirely misaligned with what the organization posting the job actually needs done.

Most organizations do not need someone to build AI. They need someone to help their existing team use it.

That is a fundamentally different job. And when the description asks for one kind of person while the organization needs the other, the hiring process filters out the right candidates before they ever have a chance to be considered.

The Resume Filter Problem

Even when a job description is written with genuine adoption and enablement in mind, the screening process is often still wired for technical signals. Whoever reviews those resumes, whether it is a recruiter, an HR professional, or an AI-assisted screening tool, has been trained to look for certain markers.

Technical certifications. Engineering titles. Implementation experience. Company names associated with AI development. These markers feel safe because they are recognizable. They feel like evidence of qualification. And they are, for a specific kind of AI work.

But the candidate who spent three years sitting beside non-technical teams, building trust, designing practical workflows, measuring whether behavior actually changed, and helping employees move from fear to fluency? That candidate's resume often looks quieter. It does not have the same technical vocabulary. It does not carry the same recognizable markers. And so it gets filtered out.

Not because the person is unqualified. Because the filter was designed for a different job.

THE INVISIBLE CANDIDATE
The most qualified person for your AI adoption role may have already applied and been screened out. Not because they lacked skill, but because their skill was invisible to a filter built for a different purpose.

Fear-Based Hiring and Why It Backfires

Another force is shaping how organizations hire for AI right now, and it deserves to be named directly. Fear.

Organizations are genuinely afraid as they navigate this transition. They are afraid of governance mistakes that expose them to legal or regulatory risk. They are concerned about security vulnerabilities arising from employees' use of AI tools without adequate oversight. They are afraid of the reputational damage caused by a highly visible AI failure. And they are afraid of appearing naive or unprepared to their boards, clients, or competitors.

When fear is driving a hiring decision, the instinct is almost always to go more technical. Technical feels safer. Technical feels controllable. Technical feels like a defensible choice if something goes wrong.

But here is what fear-based technical hiring consistently produces. It produces someone who is excellent at building and deploying systems and genuinely underprepared for the human side of the work. The training. The change management. The patient, persistent, relationship-by-relationship work of helping real people in a real organization actually changes how they do their jobs.

Technical competence does not equal adoption competence. They are different skills, different temperaments, and different kinds of work. Hiring one when you need the other does not make the organization safer. It just delays the moment when the gap becomes undeniable.

The Question That Changes Everything

Before any organization writes another AI job description, before another resume gets reviewed, there is one question that every senior leader needs to answer honestly.

What problem are we actually trying to solve?

Are you trying to build new AI systems and infrastructure? If so, you need a Builder. A technical expert who can design, deploy, and maintain AI capabilities inside your organization.

Are you trying to get your existing team to actually use the AI tools you have already purchased? If so, you need a

Trainer and an Enablement Specialist. Someone who can sit beside your employees, build workflows that fit how they actually work, address their fears, and measure whether adoption is genuinely happening.

Are you trying to align your AI strategy with your broader business goals, manage governance, and ensure your leadership team is making informed decisions? If so, you need a Strategist. Someone who understands both the technology and the organization well enough to connect them at the highest level.

These are three distinct roles. They require different skills. They attract different candidates. And they produce entirely different outcomes. Chapter 2 will give you a complete picture of each one. But the work starts here, with the willingness to ask which role you actually need before you start looking for someone to fill it.

What Happens When You Get It Right

The organizations that are seeing real AI results right now are not necessarily the ones with the largest budgets or the most sophisticated tools. They are the ones who got the role alignment right.

They hired someone whose primary skill was working with people, not systems. Someone who could walk into a department full of skeptical, busy, slightly anxious employees and, over weeks and months, help them discover that AI was not a threat but a genuinely useful tool for their daily work. Someone who could design a workflow that fits the actual rhythm of the job rather than an idealized version of it. Someone who could measure adoption not by how many licenses were active but by how many people were using the tools consistently and well.

That kind of transformation does not happen because the technology is exceptional. It happens because the right person was in the right role doing the right work.

And it starts with a job description that asks for the right things.

> *USE TOOL 2 NOW: Turn to the Appendix and find the AI Job Description Template. Before you read Chapter 2, compare the template to the last AI role your organization posted. Notice where the language differs. That difference is where the gap began.*

Continue to Chapter Two — The Three Roles Companies Confuse for One

CHAPTER TWO

The Three Roles Companies Confuse for One

One of the most consistent patterns in organizations struggling with AI adoption is a job description that reads as if it were written for three people at once. It asks for deep technical expertise. It also asks for strong communication and training skills. And somewhere near the bottom, it mentions strategic thinking and governance experience. All in one role. All for one hire.

This is not an unreasonable instinct. When organizations are navigating new territory, they want someone who can do everything. They want the person who builds the system to also explain it to employees and sit at the leadership table to help set strategy. It feels efficient. It feels comprehensive.

What it actually produces is a role that almost no one can fill authentically, a hiring process that fails in predictable ways, and an adoption gap that widens while the organization waits for a unicorn that was never coming.

Understanding the three distinct AI roles is not an academic exercise. It is the single most practical thing a senior leader can do before making another AI hiring decision.

> *Asking for all three roles in a single hire is like posting a job that requires a surgeon, a therapist, and a hospital administrator simultaneously.*

The Builder

The Builder is the person most organizations picture when they think about AI talent. This is the technical expert: the engineer, the data scientist, the systems architect who can design, build, deploy, and maintain AI infrastructure.

Builders are genuinely valuable and genuinely hard to find. They understand the technology at a deep level. They can evaluate tools, identify the right solutions for specific technical problems, and create AI capabilities that did not exist before they arrived.

What Builders are typically not is what most organizations actually need most. They are not, as a rule, skilled at sitting beside a nervous employee who has been doing their job the same way for fifteen years and patiently helping them discover that AI can make their work easier. That is not a criticism of Builders. It is simply a recognition that technical brilliance and human-centered teaching are different skills, and expecting one person to excel at both is unrealistic.

Builders are the right hire when your organization needs to create or significantly expand its AI infrastructure. They are the wrong hire when what you actually need is adoption.

The Trainer and Enablement Specialist

This is the role that is most frequently missing, most frequently misunderstood, and most urgently needed in organizations struggling with AI adoption.

The Trainer and Enablement Specialist is not a technical builder. They do not need to know how to design machine learning models or deploy AI infrastructure. What they need to know, and to be exceptionally skilled at, is how to bridge the gap between technology and the humans who need to use it.

This person designs practical AI workflows that align with how real people actually do their jobs, not with how an idealized workflow document says they should. They sit beside employees in real working sessions and build the muscle memory that makes a new tool feel natural rather than foreign. They recognize and address the emotional dimensions of AI adoption: the fear of replacement, the anxiety about making mistakes with new tools, and the quiet resistance of employees who have not been brought along on the journey with adequate care.

They measure adoption not by how many licenses are active but by how many people consistently, confidently, and well use the tools. And they stay current because, in a field where the landscape shifts every two months, the Trainer who stops learning after receiving their certification is already behind.

This role requires a rare combination of skills: genuine comfort with AI tools, the patience and communication ability of a skilled educator, and the emotional intelligence to navigate change management at a human scale. It is not a lesser role than the Builder. In most organizations right now, it is the more important one.

THE TEST FOR WHETHER YOU NEED A TRAINER

If your employees have access to AI tools but are not using them consistently, you do not have a technology problem. You have an adoption problem. And adoption problems require a Trainer, not a Builder.

The Strategist

The Strategist operates at the intersection of technology and organizational leadership. This person understands AI well enough to have an informed perspective on what is possible, and understands the organization well enough to align those possibilities with its actual goals, values, and constraints.

The Strategist handles governance. They think about ethics. They help senior leaders make informed decisions about AI investment, risk, and direction. They are not necessarily building systems or training employees, but they are the connective tissue between what AI can do and what the organization is trying to accomplish.

Many organizations need a Strategist but do not realize it until something goes wrong. An ethics exposure surfaces. A governance gap becomes a liability. Leadership realizes they have been making AI decisions without adequate strategic guidance. The Strategist is the hire that prevents those moments, or navigates them effectively when they cannot be prevented.

What Happens When You Collapse All Three

When a single job description tries to capture all three roles, a predictable series of problems follows.

First, the applicant pool becomes paradoxically smaller. There are plenty of skilled Builders, skilled Trainers, and skilled Strategists. There are very few people who are genuinely excellent at all three. The more the description demands, the fewer candidates can honestly say they qualify.

Second, the person who is eventually hired is almost always stronger in one of the three areas and weaker in the others. If they were hired through a technical screening process, they are likely strong Builders. Which means the adoption work and the strategic guidance the organization also needed are going without the skilled attention they need.

Third, the organization has no way to measure success because it never defined which of the three jobs is most important. The Builder produces technical outputs. The Trainer produces adoption metrics. The Strategist produces governance and alignment. When all three are collapsed into one role with no clear prioritization, the result is usually a lot of activity and very little clarity about whether the most important work is getting done.

The Diagnostic: Which Role Does Your Organization Actually Need?

Here is a straightforward way to think through which role your organization needs most right now.

1. **If your team does not yet have AI tools deployed and needs technical infrastructure built:** you need a Builder. Focus your job description and screening on technical credentials, deployment experience, and systems thinking.
2. **If your team has AI tools available but employees are not using them consistently or confidently:** you need a Trainer and Enablement Specialist. Focus on human-centered skills, workflow design experience, change management, and active ongoing education.
3. **If your leadership team is making AI investment decisions without adequate strategic guidance, or if governance and ethics concerns are not being systematically addressed:** you need a Strategist. Focus on organizational experience, leadership-level AI literacy, and the ability to connect technology decisions to business outcomes.

4. **If you need all three:** Do not hire one person and expect them to fill all three roles. Consider whether these can be separate hires, a phased approach, or a combination of a full-time role and consulting partnerships for the other areas.

A Critical Note on Certifications

As you evaluate candidates for any of these three roles, the question of certification will come up. It is worth understanding what AI certifications actually signal, and what they do not.

Many AI certifications are built primarily for Builders. They test technical knowledge, tool proficiency, and systems understanding. A candidate with one of these certifications may be genuinely well-qualified for a Builder role and entirely unprepared for Trainer or Strategist work.

A smaller number of certifications are designed for Trainers and Enablement Specialists. These programs cover workflow design, change management, human-centered adoption practices, AI ethics, and technical literacy. They are the ones worth looking for when you are hiring for adoption.

But the most important question about any certification is not what it covers. It is whether it is still being maintained. In a field that shifts every two months, a certification program that does not provide ongoing continuing education is producing consultants who are already working from outdated knowledge. Ask every candidate: How do you stay current? What does your ongoing training look like? The answer will tell you more than their resume credentials.

> *USE TOOL 1 NOW: Turn to the Role Clarity Diagnostic in the Appendix. This one-page assessment will help you*

identify which of the three roles your organization needs most before you post another job description.

Continue to Chapter Three — What the Gap Is Actually Costing You

CHAPTER THREE

What the Gap Is Actually Costing You

There is a version of this conversation that leans heavily on fear. It paints a picture of catastrophic consequences, of organizations left behind while competitors race ahead, of existential risk for leaders who do not act immediately.

That is not the conversation in this chapter.

What follows is a clear-eyed accounting of the costs the adoption gap imposes on organizations living with it today. Some of those costs appear in budget reports. Others are invisible until they become unavoidable. All of them are real, and all are worth understanding before deciding how to close the gap.

> *The cost of the missing role is not theoretical. It is showing up in your numbers, your culture, and your exposure.*

The Visible Costs

Unused licenses. This is the most straightforward cost to quantify, and the one most organizations are already aware of, even if they have not done the math out loud. AI tool licenses are not cheap. When those tools are available, but employees are not using them, the monthly or annual cost of each unused seat is a direct, measurable loss. Pull up your current AI tool contracts and calculate how many licenses are actively and consistently used versus how many are dormant. That number is often surprising and rarely comfortable.

Low adoption metrics. Most AI vendors provide usage data. If your organization's metrics show low engagement, infrequent logins, or surface-level use of features that barely scratch the surface of the tool's capabilities, those numbers are telling you something. The investment was made. The return is not materializing. The adoption gap is the reason.

Wasted vendor contracts. Organizations that have not achieved meaningful adoption often find themselves in renewal conversations with vendors where the honest answer is that the original investment did not deliver results. Renewing without addressing the root cause means paying again for the same outcome. Not renewing means losing access to capabilities that could be valuable if deployed correctly. Neither option is attractive.

The Invisible Costs

The visible costs are real, but they are not the whole picture. The invisible costs of the adoption gap are often larger and considerably harder to reverse.

Employee anxiety and disengagement. When AI arrives inside an organization without adequate human guidance, employees fill the silence with their own interpretations. And in the absence of clear, patient, trustworthy communication about what AI means for their roles, most employees default to fear. Fear of replacement. Fear of becoming irrelevant. Fear of making mistakes with tools they do not understand. That fear does not show up on a budget report, but it shows up in productivity, in turnover, and in the kind of quiet disengagement that is expensive and difficult to diagnose.

Ethics and governance exposure. When there is no qualified Trainer or Strategist guiding responsible AI use, employees develop their own informal practices. Some of those practices are entirely reasonable. Others create real exposure: confidential information entered into public AI tools, outputs used without adequate review, decisions influenced by AI in ways that were never disclosed or examined. These are not hypothetical risks. They are playing out within organizations right now, usually below the radar of senior leadership, and they can have legal, regulatory, and reputational consequences that are vastly more costly than getting adoption right in the first place.

Silent resistance. This may be the most costly invisible expense of all. Silent resistance occurs when employees who were never adequately brought along on the AI transition simply continue doing things the old way. They are not refusing. They are not creating conflict. They smile in meetings, nod at the right moments, then return to their desks and work exactly as they always have. The tools exist. The behavior never changed. And because the resistance is silent rather than vocal, it often goes undetected until the organization tries to measure adoption and discovers that months of investment have produced almost no meaningful change.

THE SILENT RESISTANCE TEST

Ask three frontline employees — not managers — to walk you through how they used AI tools in the last week. Their answers will tell you more about your actual adoption than any dashboard report.

The Compounding Effect

Each of these costs, visible and invisible, compounds over time. Every month that passes with the wrong person in the role, or with the right role entirely absent, the gap between where the organization is and where it needs to be grows wider and more expensive to close.

The technology keeps advancing. Employees who were uncertain about AI in the first year become more resistant in the second. The informal practices that created ethics exposure in the early months become entrenched habits that are harder to redirect. The unused licenses accumulate. The missed opportunity cost, the workflows that could have been streamlined, the hours that could have been reclaimed, the competitive advantages that could have been gained, grow larger with every passing quarter.

This is not a crisis that happens all at once. It is a slow drain that most organizations do not notice until the loss is significant.

The Question Worth Sitting With

Before moving to the next chapter, take a moment with this question.

If you added up the cost of every unused license in your organization right now, every hour spent on tasks that AI could be handling, every employee who is anxious about their role but has not been given adequate guidance, every ethics exposure that has not yet surfaced, and every month of competitive ground lost to organizations that got the adoption right, what would that number look like?

You do not need a precise figure to understand that it is significant. And you do not need a precise figure to understand that the cost of closing the gap is considerably smaller than the cost of leaving it open.

REFLECTION EXERCISE: Before reading Chapter 4, write down one visible cost and one invisible cost that you recognize in your own organization right now. Keep those two things in mind as you read the next chapter. They are the problems that Chapters 4 and 5 are going to help you solve.

Continue to Chapter Four — The Talent You Already Have

CHAPTER FOUR

The Talent You Already Have

Every major technology shift in the history of work has produced the same conversation. Jobs will be lost. Roles will be eliminated. The workforce of tomorrow will look fundamentally different from today's. And that conversation is always, to some degree, accurate.

What that conversation consistently underemphasizes is the other half of the story.

Technology shifts not only eliminate roles. They create new ones. Every disruption that has ever reduced the need for one kind of work has simultaneously increased the need for a different kind of work. The organizations that navigate these shifts most successfully are not the ones that move fastest to eliminate roles. They are the ones who move most thoughtfully to transition the people they already have into the roles the new landscape requires.

AI is not an exception to this pattern. It is the latest and most dramatic expression of it.

> *The organizations that win the AI transition are not the ones that clear the floor fastest. They are the ones who see their existing people as the raw material for the workforce AI actually needs.*

What AI Is Actually Creating

The public conversation about AI and employment tends to focus almost exclusively on what AI is taking away. The tasks it can automate. The roles it can replace. The functions that will be diminished or eliminated as the technology matures.

That conversation is real, and it deserves honest attention, which the next section of this chapter will give it. But it is incomplete without the counterpart conversation about what AI is creating.

Right now, within organizations genuinely engaged in AI adoption, new functions are emerging that did not have names eighteen months ago. Consider some of the roles that are taking shape.

- AI Workflow Designer: Someone who maps existing processes and redesigns them to incorporate AI tools effectively, ensuring the technology fits how work actually happens rather than how it looks on paper.
- AI Adoption Coach: Someone who works one-on-one and in small groups with employees to build AI fluency, address resistance, and help teams develop the habits and confidence to use AI consistently.
- Prompt Systems Specialist: Someone who develops and maintains the prompting frameworks, templates, and standards that help an organization use AI tools with consistency and quality.
- AI Ethics Reviewer: Someone who evaluates how AI is being used across the organization, identifies governance gaps, and ensures that AI practices align with the organization's values and its regulatory environment.
- AI Training Facilitator: Someone who designs and delivers ongoing learning experiences that keep employees current as the tools and best practices continue to evolve.

These are not hypothetical future roles. They are functions that organizations need right now. And the people best positioned to fill them are often not external hires with AI credentials. They are the experienced, trusted, culturally connected employees who already understand the organization, the work, and the people.

The Risk of Moving Too Fast

This is the chapter where some readers may feel a certain tension. If AI is creating new roles, why does it matter how quickly existing roles are reduced? If the workforce of tomorrow looks different from today's, why not get there as efficiently as possible?

The answer is both practical and human.

On the practical side, moving faster than your transition infrastructure can support creates a specific and costly failure mode. You reduce roles before you have trained the people who will fill the new functions. You lose institutional knowledge that cannot be documented or replaced. You create gaps in operational capacity that become visible at the worst possible moments. And you discover, usually too late, that the new roles are harder to fill from the outside than they would have been to build from within.

On the human side, organizations that are seen as moving fast and discarding people in the name of technological efficiency send a signal to their remaining workforce. That signal is: you are replaceable. When the next technology comes along, the same thing could happen to you. The response to that signal is not productivity. It is self-protection. Employees begin managing their own exposure rather than investing in the organization's success. The trust that took years to build erodes in months. And the AI transition, which was supposed to strengthen the organization, becomes the event that weakens its most important asset.

THE TRUST MULTIPLIER

Organizations that invest in transitioning their people rather than replacing them do not just protect morale — they foster innovation. They build the kind of institutional trust that makes every future transformation easier, faster, and less expensive.

What Thoughtful Transition Looks Like

Thoughtful transition begins with an honest inventory. What tasks in your organization are AI genuinely capable of absorbing right now, and in the next twelve to twenty-four months? Which roles are most affected? And critically, what new functions are those changes creating?

That inventory is not a list of people to let go. It is a map of the transition ahead. And it becomes the foundation for a different kind of conversation with your workforce: not about what is being taken away, but about where the organization is going and how it intends to bring its people along.

The next step is to identify which of your current employees have the aptitude and interest to grow into the new functions the transition is creating. This is not a trivial exercise. It requires real conversation, real observation, and real investment in learning and development. But it is an investment that pays returns in multiple directions at once: in the quality of the new functions being filled, in retaining experienced people who would otherwise be lost, and in the cultural signal it sends to everyone in the organization about how leadership handles change.

And it requires the Trainer and Enablement Specialist described in Chapter 2. Not to train employees on AI tools in a generic sense, but to guide the specific human journey of transitioning from a familiar role into a new one, with all the uncertainty, the learning curve, and the occasional frustration that journey involves.

The Conversation Employees Are Waiting For

Here is something senior leaders often underestimate: employees are not waiting for certainty about AI. They know certainty is not available. What they are waiting for is evidence that their leadership has seriously considered what this transition means for them specifically, and that there is a plan that includes them rather than one that works around them.

That conversation does not require having all the answers. It requires demonstrating that people in the organization are considered part of the solution rather than a variable to be optimized away.

The leaders who have that conversation early and back it up with genuine investment in transition and development find that their workforce becomes an asset in the AI journey rather than a source of resistance. Employees who feel seen and supported bring their institutional knowledge, their client relationships, and their operational expertise to the new functions being created. That combination, AI capability plus deep organizational knowledge, is extraordinarily hard to hire from the outside and extraordinarily powerful when developed from within.

A Word to the Leader Who Is Reading This Late

If your organization has already made decisions that moved faster than this chapter recommends, this chapter is not designed to make you feel regret. It is a chapter designed to inform your decisions ahead.

It is not too late to change the signal you are sending. It is not too late to invest in the people who remain and to make the AI transition a story about developing your workforce rather than reducing it. The organizations that recover most effectively from early missteps in this area are the ones that acknowledge the cost honestly and redirect their approach with genuine intention.

The talent you need for the AI transition may not be fully formed within your organization yet. But it is almost certainly present, waiting for someone to invest in it.

> *USE TOOL 4 NOW: Turn to the Workforce Transition Planning Guide in the Appendix. Use it to begin mapping which tasks in your organization AI is absorbing and which new functions it is creating. This exercise is worth doing before you read Chapter 5.*

Continue to Chapter Five — How to Find, Hire, and Empower the Right AI Help

CHAPTER FIVE

How to Find, Hire, and Empower the Right AI Help

Everything in this book has been leading up to this chapter. You understand the role alignment problem. You can identify the three distinct AI roles and which one your organization needs most. You know what the gap is costing you and why your existing workforce is an asset in this transition, not a liability. Now it is time to talk about what to actually do.

This chapter is practical. It is specific. It is designed to give you something you can act on before the week is out.

> *The right hire, in the right role, with the right structure around them, can change the trajectory of your AI investment faster than any tool upgrade or budget increase.*

Step One: Rewrite the Role Before You Post It

The first and most important thing you can do before hiring for any AI-related position is to go back to the diagnostic question from Chapter 1. What problem are you actually trying to solve?

If the answer is adoption, the job description needs to reflect that clearly. This means removing or deprioritizing technical credential requirements that are irrelevant to adoption work. It means explicitly asking for experience with change management, workflow design, and human-centered training. It means describing success in terms of behavior change and adoption metrics rather than technical outputs.

It also means being honest about what ongoing learning looks like for this role. A strong AI Trainer and Enablement Specialist is not someone who learned AI once and is applying that knowledge indefinitely. They are someone who is actively being re-educated as the field evolves, and the job description should reflect that expectation.

The job description template in the book's appendix will walk you through this rewrite step by step. Use it. The language matters more than most hiring managers realize, because the language of the description determines who applies, how their materials are screened, and what the role signals to the market about what your organization actually values.

Step Two: Know What You Are Actually Looking For

A rewritten job description will attract a different pool of candidates. Here is what to look for in that pool when you are hiring for an AI Trainer and Enablement Specialist.

Demonstrated experience with non-technical teams. Look for evidence that the candidate has worked with employees who were not already comfortable with AI tools. Anyone can train an early adopter. The skill that matters is the ability to build trust and fluency with the skeptical, the anxious, and the genuinely resistant.

Proof of behavior change, not just tool deployment. Ask candidates to describe a specific situation where they helped a team shift from old practices to new ones. What did the resistance look like? How did they address it? What did success look like three months later? Candidates who can answer these questions with specificity and honesty have done the real work. Candidates who give vague, positive-sounding answers probably have not.

Active, ongoing education. This is not optional. In a field that changes every two months, a candidate whose knowledge stopped growing when their certification was issued is already behind. Ask them directly what they have learned in the last sixty days. Ask them how their certification program keeps them up to date. The answer is a reliable indicator of whether they will still be genuinely effective a year from now.

Emotional intelligence and communication skills. AI adoption is fundamentally a human challenge. The person doing this work needs to be someone employees trust, someone who can hold a room through uncertainty, and someone who knows when to slow down and listen rather than push forward. These qualities are visible in conversation. Trust your observation.

The Interview Question That Changes Everything

> *If you could ask an AI consultant candidate only one question, make it this one: How do you stay current? What does your ongoing training look like?*

The answer to this question will tell you more about the candidate's real qualifications than their entire resume. A candidate who can describe a specific, structured, ongoing learning practice, a certification program that provides monthly updates, a professional community where new developments are actively discussed, and a personal discipline of testing new tools and approaches regularly, is someone whose knowledge is alive and growing.

A candidate who gives a vague answer about reading articles or keeping an eye on the news is someone whose foundational knowledge may be strong, but whose current knowledge is drifting.

In this field, drifting means falling behind. And a consultant who is falling behind cannot lead an organization forward.

Step Three: Expand Where You Are Looking

One reason organizations struggle to find strong AI Trainers and Enablement Specialists is that they look in the wrong places. The traditional job board approach is well-suited for finding Builders, people whose credentials are standardized and whose experience is relatively easy to evaluate through a resume-screening process. It is poorly designed for finding Trainers, whose most valuable qualities are relational and experiential rather than credentialed.

Consider expanding your search in these directions.

- Certification programs that specialize in AI adoption and enablement. Some programs not only train consultants in this specific area but also maintain active communities and directories of their certified graduates. A program that provides ongoing continuing education to its consultants is particularly worth engaging.
- Referrals from organizations that have already navigated successful AI adoption. If you know a peer organization that has achieved genuine adoption results, ask who did that work for them. The best AI Trainers and Enablement Specialists are almost always hired based on their results and reputation rather than through job boards.

- Consulting and workforce development partnerships. Many strong AI enablement practitioners work as independent consultants or through small firms rather than as full-time employees. A contract-to-hire arrangement or a pilot engagement can be an excellent way to evaluate fit before making a permanent commitment.
- Internal talent with development investment. As discussed in Chapter 4, some of your most effective AI adoption support may come from existing employees who have been developed for this function. This is particularly true for the Adoption Coach role, where cultural familiarity and existing relationships are genuine assets.

Step Four: Evaluate the Certification

When a candidate presents an AI certification, it is worth taking a moment to understand what it covers and whether it is still current. The questions in Tool 5 of the appendix will help you do this systematically, but here are the most important ones.

- Does the program cover change management and human adoption practices, or is it primarily technical?
- Does the program address AI ethics and governance alongside proficiency with tools?
- Does the program provide ongoing continuing education, or did the learning stop at the point of certification?
- How frequently is the curriculum updated to reflect changes in the field?
- Is the certifying organization itself active and current, or has it remained static since its founding?

A certification from a program that cannot answer these questions confidently is a credential that tells you relatively little about whether the candidate is equipped to do the work you actually need done.

Step Five: Structure the Relationship for Success

Even the right hire will struggle without the right structure. The most common failure mode after a good hiring decision is the absence of clear expectations, adequate access, and a meaningful feedback loop.

Define success in adoption terms. Before the person starts, agree on what success looks like at 30, 60, and 90 days. Frame those metrics around behavior change and adoption rather than activity. Not how many training sessions were delivered, but how many employees are consistently using the tools. Not how many workflows were designed, but how many are being used in practice.

Give them access to leadership. AI adoption work touches every level of the organization. A Trainer who is empowered only to work with frontline employees but cannot gain traction with managers or leadership will be limited in what they can achieve. The most effective AI adoption work happens with visible, active support from the top.

Create a real feedback loop. The person doing adoption work will see things that are not visible at the leadership level: where resistance is concentrated, where the tools do not fit the workflow, and where employees have questions that are not being answered. Build a regular, honest feedback channel between this person and leadership.

Treat this as a long-term investment. Sustainable AI adoption does not happen in ninety days. The organizations that achieve the most durable results are those that commit to this work over multiple years, evolving their approach as tools evolve and the workforce continues to grow in its AI fluency. The first hire is the beginning of a capability, not a one-time fix.

USE TOOL 3 NOW: Turn to the Candidate Evaluation Checklist in the Appendix. Use it to prepare for your next AI consultant or Trainer interview. The checklist includes the questions that will tell you what a resume cannot.

Continue to Conclusion — The Gap Is Closable. If You Move Now.

CONCLUSION

The Gap Is Closable. If You Move Now.

You have read this far because something in this book reminded you of something you already knew. The pattern described in these pages, the misaligned job description, the wrong role in the wrong function, the employees who were never adequately brought along, the costs accumulating quietly beneath the surface, is not a theoretical scenario. It is playing out inside your organization right now. Or it was. Or you are determined to make sure it does not.

Whatever brought you here, you are leaving with something you did not have before. Clarity. The clarity to name the problem accurately. The framework to understand what kind of help you actually need. The tools to act on that understanding before the week is out.

> *The missing role is no longer a mystery. You know what it looks like, where to find it, and what it costs to leave the gap open any longer.*

What Changes Now

When you close this book, a few things should be different.

The next AI job description your organization writes will be built around the actual problem you are trying to solve, not around a checklist of technical credentials borrowed from a role that was designed for a different purpose. It will ask for the skills that adoption work actually requires. And it will signal to the market that your organization understands the difference between building AI and helping humans use it.

The next AI candidate you evaluate will be asked the question that matters most: how do you stay current? The answer to that question will tell you whether you are looking at someone whose knowledge is alive and growing or someone who learned AI once and has been working from that foundation ever since.

The conversation about your existing workforce will be different. Instead of asking which roles AI will eliminate, you will also be asking which new functions AI is creating and which of your current employees are the right people to grow into them. That is a different conversation. It produces different decisions. And it sends a different signal to your workforce about what kind of organization you are.

The Leaders Who Will Win This Transition

The organizations that come out of this moment stronger are not the ones with the largest AI budgets or the most sophisticated tools. They are the ones with the clearest understanding of what the transition actually requires at the human level.

They are the ones that hired for adoption rather than for impressiveness. The ones that invested in their existing people rather than racing to replace them. The ones that built feedback loops that surfaced what was actually happening on the ground rather than relying on dashboard metrics that looked better than reality. The ones that treated AI adoption as a long-term cultural shift rather than a short-term implementation project.

Those organizations are not rare. They are not uniquely gifted or specially resourced. They made different choices earlier because their leaders had the clarity to see the problem accurately and the courage to act on what they saw.

You have that clarity now.

The Partnership That Makes It Real

One final thought before you turn to the toolkit.

The ideas in this book are useful. The tools in the appendix are practical. But the real transformation happens when organizations connect with the right people to do this work. That means finding AI Trainers and Enablement Specialists who are genuinely equipped for it, certified by programs that take ongoing education seriously, and experienced in the human-centered work that real adoption requires.

A growing community of these professionals exists. They are out there. They are trained, current, and ready to do the work your organization needs done. The gap described in this book exists in part because senior leaders have not known how to find them or how to recognize them when they did. The tools in this appendix are designed to close that gap.

Use them this week. Not next quarter. This week.

Your team is watching how you handle this moment. They want to succeed in a world that includes AI. They are not opposed to change. They are waiting for someone to lead them through it with clarity, competence, and genuine care for the people on the other side of the transition.

That leadership starts with the role that has been missing.

Now you know what it is. Go find it.

APPENDIX

The Leader's AI Hiring Toolkit

The following tools are designed to be used, not just read. Each one corresponds to a specific action step referenced in the chapters of this book. Pull them out. Write on them. Share them with your team. They are yours to use as many times as you need them.

Tool 1: The Role Clarity Diagnostic

Use this diagnostic before writing any AI job description. Answer each question honestly. Your answers will tell you which of the three AI roles your organization actually needs most right now.

Section A: Where Is Your Organization in the AI Journey?

☐ We have not yet deployed AI tools and need the technical infrastructure built.

☐ We have AI tools available, but employees are not using them consistently.

☐ We have adoption happening, but lack strategic guidance and governance.

☐ We have all three challenges and need to prioritize.

Section B: What Does Success Look Like in 90 Days?

☐ New AI systems or capabilities are deployed and functioning. (Points to Builder)

☐ Measurably more employees are using AI tools consistently and confidently. (Points to Trainer)

☐ Leadership is making AI decisions with clear strategic alignment and governance. (Points to Strategist)

Section C: What Is the Primary Complaint Right Now?

☐ We do not have the technical capability to do what we want to do with AI.

☐ We have the tools, but people are not using them.

☐ We are not sure if our AI efforts are aligned with our actual business goals.

☐ We are worried about ethics and governance exposure.

Your Role Clarity Result

If most of your answers point to technical capability gaps, prioritize hiring a Builder.

If most of your answers point to unused tools and low adoption, prioritize hiring a Trainer and Enablement Specialist.

If most of your answers point to gaps in strategy, governance, or alignment, prioritize hiring a Strategist.

If your answers point to all three, use this diagnostic to rank your priorities and plan a phased approach rather than trying to hire one person for all three roles.

Tool 2: The AI Job Description Template

This template is designed for organizations hiring an AI Trainer and Enablement Specialist, the role most commonly missing from organizations struggling with adoption. Adapt the language to fit your organization's voice and culture.

Position Title

AI Adoption and Enablement Specialist

Alternative titles: AI Workforce Trainer — AI Transition Coach — AI Enablement Lead

What This Role Is

We are looking for someone whose primary skill is helping real people in a real organization learn to use AI tools confidently and consistently. This is not a technical build role. It is a human-centered change management role that requires deep familiarity with AI tools, genuine skill at teaching and coaching, and the patience and emotional intelligence to guide employees through a meaningful transition.

What You Will Do

☐ Design practical AI workflows that fit how our team actually works, not how an idealized process document says they should.

☐ Work directly with employees at all levels to build AI fluency, address resistance, and develop the habits that make AI tools a natural part of daily work.

☐ Measure adoption through behavioral indicators, not just license activity, and report honestly on what is working and what is not.

☐ Stay actively current in a rapidly evolving field and bring relevant new developments to our team as they emerge.

☐ Collaborate with leadership to identify where AI can reduce friction, save time, and create capacity for higher-value work.

What We Are Looking For

☐ Demonstrated experience helping non-technical teams adopt new tools or practices.

☐ Evidence of behavior change, not just tool deployment, in prior work.

☐ An active, structured approach to ongoing learning in the AI field.

☐ Strong communication, coaching, and relationship-building skills.

☐ Familiarity with AI tools, including but not limited to (list your specific tools here).

☐ Certification from a program that includes ongoing continuing education is preferred.

What We Are Not Looking For

We are not looking for a software engineer or AI developer for this role. Technical depth is less important than human-centered skill. Candidates who are primarily builders or architects should explore our other open roles.

How We Will Measure Success

Success in this role is measured by adoption metrics, not activity metrics. At 90 days, we expect to see measurable increases in consistent tool usage across the teams this person supports. At 6 months, we expect documented workflow improvements and qualitative evidence of reduced employee anxiety around AI. At 12 months, we expect AI to be a natural part of how our team works rather than an initiative people are aware of but not engaged with.

Tool 3: The Candidate Evaluation Checklist

Use this checklist when interviewing AI consultants and Enablement Specialist candidates. The questions are designed to surface what a resume cannot show.

Before the Interview: Resume Review

☐ Does the resume describe outcomes (behavior change, adoption results) rather than only activities (trainings delivered, tools deployed)?

☐ Is there evidence of work with non-technical employees, not just technically skilled teams?

☐ Does the candidate's certification background indicate ongoing learning, or a single point-in-time credential?

☐ Are the AI tools and practices described on the resume current, or do they reflect the state of the field from a year or more ago?

During the Interview: Essential Questions

1. Tell me about a time you helped a team adopt a new tool or practice that they were initially resistant to. What did the resistance look like, and how did you address it?
2. How do you stay current in the AI field? What does your ongoing training look like, and what have you learned in the last sixty days?
3. Describe a workflow you designed for a non-technical team. How did you figure out what they actually needed versus what you initially thought they needed?
4. How do you measure whether adoption is actually happening, as opposed to measuring whether training was delivered?
5. Tell me about a situation where an AI rollout you were involved in did not go as planned. What happened, and what did you do?
6. What does responsible AI use look like in a workplace setting? How have you addressed ethics and governance in your prior work?

What Strong Answers Look Like

Strong candidates answer with specificity. They name the actual resistance they encountered, describe the actual steps they took, and report the actual outcomes, honestly noting what worked and what did not. They can speak fluently about what they have learned recently because they are actively learning. They treat ethics and governance as genuinely important rather than as a box to check.

Weaker candidates give vague, positive answers that sound good but lack the specificity of real experience. They describe AI adoption as straightforward. They struggle to articulate how they measure behavioral change. And they respond to the ongoing learning question with generalities rather than specifics.

Tool 4: The Workforce Transition Planning Guide

Use this guide to begin mapping how AI is changing the work in your organization and how you can invest in your existing people rather than simply reducing headcount.

Step 1. Map the Shifting Tasks. List the tasks in your organization that AI is currently capable of absorbing, or will be capable of absorbing in the next 12 to 24 months. Be specific — not just administrative work, but the particular reports, communications, summaries, analyses, or routine decisions that AI can handle.

Step 2. Identify the New Functions. For each shifting task, ask: what new work does this create? If AI handles the initial drafting of a document, someone still needs to review it, refine it, and apply judgment. List every new function the shift creates.

Step 3. Assess Your Current Workforce. Which of your current employees have the aptitude, the interest, or the foundational skills to grow into those new functions with adequate development investment? Look at their capabilities, curiosity, and track record of adaptation.

Step 4. Design the Development Path. For each employee you identify, design a specific development path. What training? What mentoring? What hands-on practice with AI tools? What does success look like at six and twelve months?

Step 5. Communicate with Clarity and Care. Before you implement any of this, have a real conversation with your workforce about where the organization is going and how it intends to bring people along. Employees who feel included become assets in the transition. Employees who receive a memo become a source of resistance.

Tool 5: Questions to Ask Any AI Certification Program

Before trusting that a candidate's AI certification reflects current, relevant, human-centered expertise, ask the certifying organization these questions directly. A credible program will have clear, confident answers.

1. What does your curriculum cover beyond technical tool proficiency? Specifically, does it address change management, human-centered adoption, and AI ethics?
2. How frequently is your curriculum updated to reflect changes in the AI field?
3. Do you provide ongoing continuing education to certified graduates, or does the learning stop at the point of certification?
4. What does your continuing education program look like? How often are updates provided, and what format do they take?
5. How do you ensure that your certified graduates are staying current with developments in the field?
6. Can you provide examples of the kinds of outcomes your certified graduates have produced in real organizational settings?

7. Does your program distinguish between different types of AI roles – such as Builders, Trainers, and Strategists – or does it treat all AI work as a single category?
8. What is your approach to AI ethics and governance within the certification curriculum?
9. How do you evaluate whether someone is genuinely ready to do adoption and enablement work, as opposed to technical work?
10. What does your community of certified graduates look like? Is it an active, ongoing professional community, or a credential without a community?

ABOUT THE AUTHOR

Chauntelle Ricks is a Certified AI Strategist, founder of Edge Effect AI, and author of Future Proof. Her work sits at the intersection of technology and the humans who need to use it, helping organizations close the gap between AI investment and real, measurable results.

Her approach was shaped by a moment she describes as the turning point in her work. Shortly after completing her AI certification, she reviewed her newly earned material and realized the landscape had already shifted. Tools had been updated. Best practices had evolved. That experience became the foundation for everything she teaches: that in a field that changes every two months, the commitment to ongoing learning is the credential that matters most.

Chauntelle works with corporate teams, learning and development leaders, and executives who are ready to turn their AI investment into real adoption. She speaks at conferences, leads workshops, and delivers training engagements that equip leaders and their teams to navigate the AI transition with clarity, confidence, and genuine care for the people on the other side of the change.

She is also at work on a growing series of books bringing the same human-centered framework to specific industries, including real estate, healthcare, financial services, and education, as well as a guide for students and parents navigating a world being reshaped by artificial intelligence.

To book Chauntelle for speaking, training, or corporate engagements:

ccharisseai@gmail.com

THE MISSING ROLE

The Leadership Gap Standing Between Your Team and Real AI Results

For speaking inquiries, bulk orders, and corporate training:
ccharisseai@gmail.com

Additional Resources:
https://stan.store/edgeeffectai

Transforming Glory Publishing Group
ISBN: 978-1-962942-12-6

Made in the USA
Monee, IL
05 November 2026

67813123R00036